I0448898

June 2013

PROGRAM EVALUATION

Strategies to Facilitate Agencies' Use of Evaluation in Program Management and Policy Making

GAO-13-570

June 2013

GAO Highlights

Highlights of GAO-13-570, a report to congressional committees

PROGRAM EVALUATION

Strategies to Facilitate Agencies' Use of Evaluation in Program Management and Policy Making

Why GAO Did This Study

The GPRA Modernization Act of 2010 (GPRAMA) aims to ensure that agencies use performance information in decision making and holds them accountable for achieving results and improving government performance. GPRAMA requires GAO to evaluate the act's implementation; this report is one of a series to assess its initial implementation. GAO examined the extent of agencies' use of program evaluations—a particular form of performance information, factors that may hinder their use in program management and policy making, and strategies that may facilitate their use.

GAO surveyed a stratified random sample of 4,391 federal civilian managers and supervisors to obtain their perspectives on several results-oriented management topics, including the extent of and barriers to their evaluation use. GAO also interviewed the Office of Management and Budget and evaluators on barriers to evaluation use and strategies to facilitate it at five agencies selected for their evaluation experience in the Departments of Agriculture, Health and Human Services, and Labor. These officials' views cannot be generalized but provide useful insights.

What GAO Recommends

GAO is not making recommendations.

The Departments of Agriculture, Health and Human Services, and Labor, and Office of Management and Budget staff provided technical comments on a draft of this report that we incorporated as appropriate.

View GAO-13-570. For more information, contact Nancy Kingsbury at KingsburyN@gao.gov, 202-512-2700

What GAO Found

In a governmentwide survey, GAO found that most federal managers lack recent evaluations of their programs. Thirty-seven percent reported that an evaluation had been completed within the past 5 years of any program, operation, or project they were involved in. Another 40 percent of managers reported that they did not know if an evaluation had been completed. However, 80 percent of managers who did have evaluations reported that those evaluations contributed to a moderate or greater extent to improving program management or performance and to assessing program effectiveness or value. Fewer reported that evaluations contributed moderately or more to allocating resources within a program (67 percent) or streamlining programs (61 percent).

Of the 37 percent of federal managers who had evaluations, the factor most often rated as having hindered use to a great or very great extent was lack of resources to implement the evaluation findings (33 percent). The next most frequently reported barriers related to program context, such as resolving differences of opinion among program stakeholders (23 percent). Other issues were not considered significant barriers by these managers, such as the lack of credibility or timeliness of study results, lack of leadership commitment or support for using evaluations, or difficulty accepting unexpected findings. Managers reported limited knowledge of congressional support for using results; 39 percent reported not being able to judge whether this was a barrier.

The agency evaluators GAO interviewed noted that it usually takes a number of studies, rather than just one, to influence change in programs or policies. They described using evaluations to modify existing or develop new programs and share what works with their program partners. They emphasized three basic strategies to facilitate evaluation influence:

1. Demonstrate leadership support of evaluation for accountability and improvement by promoting capacity building and the use of evidence and funding evaluation offices to promote and support the use of evidence.

2. Build a strong body of evidence by attending to rigor in whatever methods are used and accumulating a knowledge base from which to respond to varied questions over time or fast-breaking policy discussions.

3. Engage stakeholders throughout the evaluation process—developing relationships to gain their input to planning and buy-in; providing assistance, training, and incentives; and disseminating usable messages.

GAO observes that

- Agencies' lack of evaluations may be the greatest barrier to their informing program managers and policy makers.
- Seeking out in advance the interests and concerns of program stakeholders, including Congress, can help ensure that evaluations will provide the information necessary for effective management and oversight.
- Comprehensive evaluations that examine the coverage and effectiveness of federal programs and policies aimed at achieving similar outcomes could be key to coordinating and streamlining programs to reduce duplication and overlap.

_____ United States Government Accountability Office

Contents

Abbreviations

ACF	Administration for Children and Families
ASPE	Office of the Assistant Secretary for Planning and Evaluation
CDC	Centers for Disease Control and Prevention
CEO	Chief Evaluation Office
DDT	Division of Diabetes Translation
DHAP	Division of HIV/AIDS Prevention
DPP	Diabetes Prevention Program
ETA	Employment and Training Administration
FNS	Food and Nutrition Service
GPRA	Government Performance and Results Act of 1993
GPRAMA	GPRA Modernization Act of 2010
HHS	U.S. Department of Health and Human Services
OADPG	Office of the Associate Director for Program
OMB	Office of Management and Budget
OPDR	Office of Policy Development and Research
OPRE	Office of Planning, Research, and Evaluation
OPS	Office of Policy Support
PART	Program Assessment Rating Tool
PEPFAR	President's Plan for AIDS Relief
PHS	Public Health Service
SES	Senior Executive Service
SNAP	Supplemental Nutrition Assistance Program
TANF	Temporary Assistance for Needy Families
USDA	U.S. Department of Agriculture
WIC	Special Supplemental Nutrition Program for Women, Infants, and Children

U.S. GOVERNMENT ACCOUNTABILITY OFFICE

441 G St. N.W.
Washington, DC 20548

June 26, 2013

The Honorable Tom Carper
Chairman
The Honorable Tom Coburn
Ranking Member
Committee on Homeland Security and Governmental Affairs
United States Senate

The Honorable Elijah E. Cummings
Ranking Member
Committee on Oversight and Government Reform
House of Representatives

The federal government faces a number of significant fiscal, management, and performance challenges. In the absence of policy change, rapid growth in federal government debt will increasingly constrain budgetary flexibility and the ability to address current and future needs. Tough choices will be required to reform programs and management activities to reduce costs and better link resources to results. The reporting requirements of the Government Performance and Results Act of 1993 (GPRA) were intended to provide both congressional and executive decision makers with more objective information on the relative effectiveness and efficiency of federal programs and spending.[1] Although GPRA helped improve the availability of agency performance information, in our previous surveys, about half of federal managers reported using performance data for decision making to a great or very great extent.[2]

The GPRA Modernization Act of 2010 (GPRAMA) aims to ensure that agencies use performance information in decision making and holds them accountable for achieving results and improving government performance.[3] The Office of Management and Budget (OMB), too, has

---

[1]Pub. L. No. 103-62, 107 Stat. 285 (1993).

[2]GAO, *Government Performance: Lessons Learned for the Next Administration on Using Performance Information to Improve Results,* GAO-08-1026T (Washington, D.C.: July 24, 2008).

[3]Pub. L. No. 111-352, 124 Stat. 3866 (2011).

encouraged agencies to improve government effectiveness by increasing their use of evidence and rigorous program evaluation in making budget, management, and policy decisions. GPRAMA requires GAO to evaluate the act's implementation at several junctures; this report is one of a series responding to the mandate to assess its initial implementation by June 30, 2013. The report addresses agencies' access to and use of evaluation studies—a particular form of program performance information—for decisions.

Our objectives were to identify

1. the extent to which federal agencies are using program evaluations in selected program management and policy making activities;

2. factors, if any, that hinder agencies' use of evaluation in program management and policy making; and

3. factors or strategies that facilitate evaluation use.

To address our objectives, we surveyed a stratified random sample of 4,391 persons from a population of approximately 148,300 civilian managers and supervisors working in the 24 executive branch agencies covered by the Chief Financial Officers Act of 1990. The questionnaire was designed to obtain the observations and perceptions of respondents on various aspects of such results-oriented management topics as the presence and use of performance measures, hindrances to measuring performance and using performance information, and program evaluation use. The web-based survey was administered between November 2012 and February 2013. About 69 percent of the eligible sample responded with usable questionnaires. The sample allowed us to generalize our results to the governmentwide population of federal managers. (See appendix I for more information on the survey.) We further discuss the survey's results in a June 2013 report summarizing our body of work on the implementation of GPRAMA and in an electronic supplement showing the responses to all survey items at the governmentwide and individual agency levels.[4]

In addition, we interviewed OMB staff and evaluation officials at five federal agencies on factors or strategies that have hindered or facilitated these agencies' use of evaluation results in decision making. Selected for their experience with evaluation, these agencies were the Food and Nutrition Service (FNS) at the U.S. Department of Agriculture (USDA), the Administration for Children and Families (ACF) and the Centers for Disease Control and Prevention (CDC) at the U.S. Department of Health and Human Services (HHS), and the Employment and Training Administration (ETA) and Chief Evaluation Office (CEO) at the U.S. Department of Labor. To identify agencies meeting our criteria, we reviewed previous GAO reports and agency documents for evidence of emphasis on conducting evaluations. For example, we searched for examples of agencies' incorporating the results of program evaluations in their strategic plans. We cannot generalize this information governmentwide but we believe it supplements and clarifies the survey results and provides useful strategies that other agencies can adapt.

We conducted this performance audit from September 2012 to June 2013 in accordance with generally accepted government auditing standards. Those standards require that we plan and perform the audit to obtain sufficient, appropriate evidence to provide a reasonable basis for our findings and conclusions based on our audit objectives. We believe that the evidence obtained provides a reasonable basis for our findings and conclusions based on our audit objectives.

---

[4]For the report, see GAO, *Managing for Results: Executive Branch Should More Fully Implement the GPRA Modernization Act to Address Pressing Governance Challenges,* GAO-13-518 (Washington, D.C.: June 26, 2013); for the e-supplement, see GAO, *Managing for Results: 2013 Federal Managers Survey on Organizational Performance and Management Issues,* GAO-13-519SP (Washington, D.C.: June 2013). Other reports pursuant to this mandate include GAO, *Managing for Results: GAO's Work Related to the Interim Crosscutting Priority Goals under the GPRA Modernization Act,* GAO-12-620R (Washington, D.C.: May 31, 2012); *Managing for Results: Data-Driven Performance Reviews Show Promise but Agencies Should Explore How to Involve Other Relevant Agencies,* GAO-13-228 (Washington, D.C.: Feb. 27, 2013); *Managing for Results: Agencies Have Elevated Performance Management Roles, but Additional Training Is Needed,* GAO-13-356 (Washington, D.C.: Apr. 16, 2013); *Managing for Results: Agencies Should More Fully Develop Priority Goals under the GPRA Modernization Act,* GAO-13-174 (Washington, D.C.: Apr. 19, 2013); and *Managing for Results: Leading Practices Should Guide the Continued Development of Performance.gov,* GAO-13-517 (Washington, D.C.: June 6, 2013).

Background

Program evaluations are systematic studies that use research methods to address specific questions about program performance.[5] Evaluation is closely related to performance measurement and reporting. Whereas performance measurement entails the ongoing monitoring and reporting of program progress toward preestablished goals, program evaluation typically assesses the achievement of a program's objectives and other aspects of performance in the context in which the program operates. In particular, evaluations can be designed to isolate the causal impacts of programs from other external economic or environmental conditions in order to assess a program's effectiveness. Thus, an evaluation study can provide a valuable supplement to ongoing performance reporting by measuring results that are too difficult or expensive to assess annually, explaining the reasons why performance goals were not met, or assessing whether one approach is more effective than another.

Evaluation can play a key role in program planning, management, and oversight by providing feedback on both program design and execution to program managers, legislative and executive branch policy officials, and the public. The program evaluation literature has identified different ways that program managers and policy makers can use evaluation results to (1) clarify understanding of how the program does or does not address a problem of interest, (2) make changes to improve the design or management of an existing program or policy, (3) support or change resource allocations within or across programs, (4) share promising practices or lessons learned with service providers or program partners, or (5) improve the quality of program or policy assessment.[6]

In addition, the program evaluation literature has identified influences on whether evaluation results are used for decision making such as (1) characteristics of the evaluation study (for example, quality and relevance), (2) agency evaluation capacity (skills and understanding), (3)

---

[5]GPRAMA defines program evaluation as an assessment, through objective measurement and systematic analysis, of the manner and extent to which federal programs achieve intended objectives; see 31 U.S.C. § 1115(h)(12).

[6]Harry P. Hatry, Elaine Morley, Shelli B. Rossman, and Joseph S. Wholey, *How Federal Programs Use Outcome Information: Opportunities for Federal Managers* (Washington, D.C.: IBM Endowment for the Business of Government, 2003). For a broader discussion of the social process of policy deliberation and ways that science findings and theories may contribute to that discussion, see also Kenneth Prewitt, Thomas A. Schwandt, and Miron L. Straf, eds., *Using Science as Evidence in Public Policy* (Washington, D.C.: National Academies Press, 2012).

policy context of decision making, and (4) stakeholder involvement in the evaluation. For example, our recent reviews of evaluations of programs funded under the President's Plan for AIDS Relief (PEPFAR) and programs supporting education in science, technology, engineering, and mathematics concluded that limitations in evaluation quality, planning, and dissemination were barriers to the use of study results.[7]

Our Interviews at Health and Human Services Agencies

In HHS, we interviewed officials at ACF and CDC because of their mature evaluation experience and officials from the Office of the Assistant Secretary for Planning and Evaluation (ASPE) because they coordinate HHS's evaluation, research, and demonstration activities and report to the Congress on its evaluations. ASPE conducts some studies on cross-cutting issues but primarily relies on other agencies to evaluate their own programs.

Administration for Children and Families

ACF oversees and helps finance programs to improve the social and economic well-being of families, individuals, and communities—the Head Start program is an example. ACF also assists Temporary Assistance for Needy Families (TANF) as well as state programs for child support enforcement. The principal office for managing evaluation at ACF is the Office of Planning, Research, and Evaluation (OPRE), which also provides guidance, analysis, technical assistance, and oversight related to strategic planning, performance measurement, research, and evaluation methods. OPRE conducts statistical, policy, and program analyses and synthesizes and disseminates research and demonstration findings. It consults with outside groups on ideas that feed into program and evaluation planning, including researchers, program partners, and other content area experts.

Centers for Disease Control and Prevention

CDC is charged with protecting the public health by developing and providing to persons and communities information and tools for preventing and controlling disease, promoting health, and preparing for new health threats. Some evaluation activities are funded by the Public Health Service (PHS) evaluation set-aside; in 2012, the Secretary of

---

[7]GAO, *Science, Technology, Engineering, and Mathematics Education: Strategic Planning Needed to Better Manage Overlapping Programs across Multiple Agencies*, GAO-12-108 (Washington, D.C.: Jan. 20, 2012), and *President's Emergency Plan for AIDS Relief: Agencies Can Enhance Evaluation Quality, Planning, and Dissemination*, GAO-12-673 (Washington, D.C.: May 31, 2012).

Health and Human Services was authorized to use up to 2.5 percent of appropriations for programs authorized by the PHS Act for evaluating the implementation and effectiveness of those programs.[8] The set-aside is also used to fund databases of the National Center for Health Statistics and programs that cut across CDC's divisions. Presently, the divisions within CDC control most of the evaluation funding that is focused on their respective programs. In 2010, CDC created the Office of the Associate Director for Program (OADPG) [sic] to promote program improvement through evidence-based practice. Among other duties, the office provides CDC-wide direction, standardization, and technical assistance for program planning, performance and accountability, and evaluation.

In addition to interviews with OADPG, we interviewed evaluation staff from CDC's Division of HIV/AIDS Prevention (DHAP) and from the National Diabetes Prevention Program (National DPP) in the Division of Diabetes Translation (DDT) to discuss their use of evaluations. DHAP is charged with preventing HIV infection and reducing the incidence of HIV-related illness and death. DHAP provides national leadership and support for HIV prevention research and for developing, implementing, and evaluating evidence-based HIV prevention programs. It also conducts surveillance and tests biomedical interventions to reduce HIV transmission and progression. The Division of Diabetes Translation focuses on translating science into everyday practice. For example, the National Diabetes Prevention Program promotes evidence-based lifestyle change programs to prevent type 2 diabetes. The National DPP is a public-private partnership of community organizations, insurers, employers, health care organizations, and government agencies designed to help establish a network of structured, evidence-based lifestyle change programs for people at high risk for the disease.

Our Interviews at Labor Agencies

Labor's ETA plays an important role in providing job training, employment assistance, and labor market information and income maintenance services primarily through state and local workforce development systems. The Office of Policy Development and Research (OPDR) provides ETA with strategic approaches to improve performance and outcomes through research, demonstrations, and the evaluation of major

---

[8]Consolidated Appropriations Act, 2012, Pub. L. No. 112-174, division F, title II, § 205, 125 Stat. 786, 1082 (2011).

ETA programs. In addition to ETA's staff, we interviewed staff from Labor's Chief Evaluation Office. Labor established the Chief Evaluation Officer position in 2010 within its Office of the Assistant Secretary for Policy to manage and coordinate Labor's evaluation agenda.[9] The Chief Evaluation Office supports a wide range of high-priority and special research and evaluation activities across the department. To foster research relevant to policy, these activities include developing designs and proposed methodology (experimental as well as nonexperimental designs), collecting and analyzing data, maintaining information systems, developing reports, convening meetings, and briefing federal executive and other staff.

Our Interviews at Agriculture Agencies

FNS works within USDA's Food, Nutrition, and Consumer Services to end hunger and obesity, administering 15 federal nutrition assistance programs, including the Supplemental Nutrition Assistance Program (SNAP), and school meals. FNS conducts a variety of studies, evaluations, and related activities to meet nutrition assistance program goals. Its Office of Policy Support (OPS) conducts program analysis and assessment to inform the policymaking and management of federal nutrition assistance. OPS is FNS's coordinating point for program-related nutrition and policy services, working to coordinate its strategic and operational planning processes; its multidisciplinary staff analyze and evaluate key policy and program issues for the Congress and the public.

---

[9]In 2010 and 2011 we recommended improvements to ETA's research planning and dissemination, which the agency agreed with and is in the process of implementing. See GAO, *Employment and Training Administration: Increased Authority and Accountability Could Improve Research Program*, GAO-10-243 (Washington, D.C.: Jan. 29, 2010), and *Employment and Training Administration: More Actions Needed to Improve Transparency and Accountability of Its Research Program*, GAO-11-285 (Washington, D.C.: Mar. 15, 2011).

GAO-13-570 Agency Use of Evaluation

Federal Managers Reported That, Where Available, Evaluations Had Helped Improve Programs

Most Managers Lacked Recent Evaluations of Their Programs

Our governmentwide survey of federal managers found that the majority did not have recent evaluations of their programs. Just over a third (37 percent) reported that an evaluation had been completed in the past 5 years on any program, operation, or project they were involved in. Significantly more Senior Executive Service (SES) managers reported having had evaluations than non-SES managers (54 percent versus 36 percent). This should be expected, since SES managers are likely to oversee a broader range of programs than non-SES managers, any one of which might have been evaluated.

Moreover, a similar number of federal managers (40 percent) reported that *they did not know* if an evaluation had been completed. We believe, for three reasons, that this may represent midlevel staff's lack of familiarity with activities outside their programs rather than their problems in understanding the definition of "program evaluation." First, in the fairly broad definition of evaluation we provided in the survey, we included both implementation and outcome or effectiveness evaluation. Second, many more non-SES managers than SES managers reported not knowing if there had been an evaluation (41 percent compared to 24 percent). Third, in other questions in our survey about GPRAMA provisions, larger proportions of midlevel managers reported that they had not heard of GPRAMA (21 percent of SES, 50 percent of non-SES managers) or were not familiar with any of the cross-agency priority goals it requires OMB, in coordination with agencies, to establish (26 percent of SES, 41 percent of non-SES managers).

Of the 37 percent of managers who had evaluations, almost all (90 percent) reported that the agency or program itself conducted or contracted for these evaluations. Many of these managers also reported that studies had been conducted by their Inspector General or GAO (46 and 38 percent, respectively) or others such as independent boards or commissions (23 percent). Because of variation in the responsibilities of federal managers, we cannot deduce from these results how many programs have been evaluated. However, even had additional evaluations been conducted by others within or outside an agency, if managers were unaware of them, their results would not have been available for use.

Most Managers Who Had Evaluations Reported That Evaluations Helped Them Assess and Improve Programs

For the 37 percent of federal managers who had evaluations, the survey asked to what extent those evaluations had contributed to a variety of program management and policy making activities. Eighty to 81 percent of these managers reported that evaluations contributed to a moderate or greater extent to implementing changes to improve program management or performance and in assessing program effectiveness or value. Fewer managers reported that evaluations contributed to resource allocation or informing the public. Figure 1 summarizes their responses to the 11 activities the survey posed.

Figure 1: Managers Who Had Evaluations Report on the Extent to Which They Contributed to 11 Program Activities

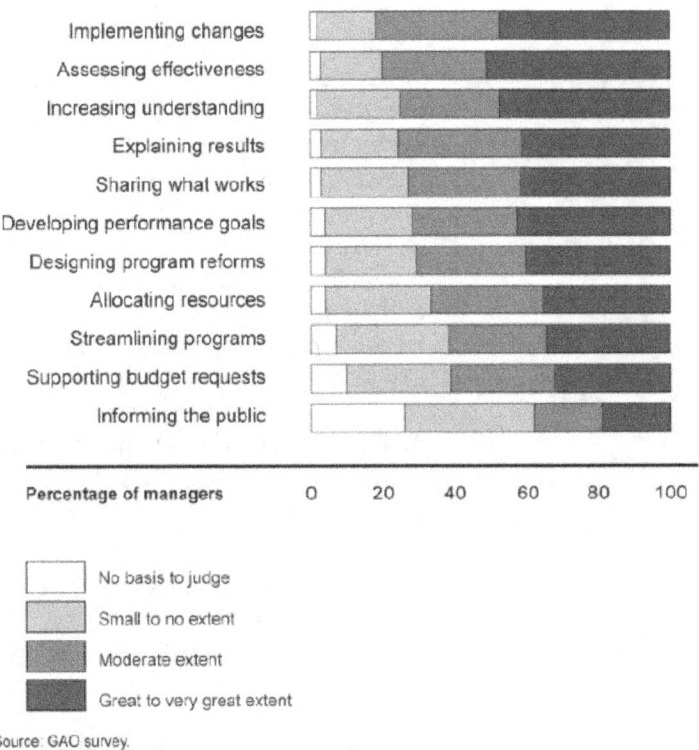

Source: GAO survey.

Note: These percentages are based on the response of managers who reported having program evaluations completed within the past 5 years.

Managers reported that evaluations had contributed to a *moderate or greater extent* to their taking direct actions to improve programs such as

- implementing changes to improve program management or performance (81 percent),
- sharing what works with others (73 percent),
- developing or revising performance goals (72 percent), and
- designing or supporting program reforms (71 percent).

They reported that evaluations had to a *lesser extent* helped them

- streamline programs to reduce duplicative activities (61 percent).

The evaluators we interviewed provided several examples of how evaluations had contributed to their modifying existing or developing new programs. For example, the FNS evaluators stated that conducting a series of cost-effectiveness studies had led to replacing paper coupons with electronic benefit cards in the Supplemental Nutrition Assistance Program (previously, food stamps).

CDC, too, led the design of the lifestyle change diabetes prevention program for persons at high risk of developing type 2 diabetes based on a systematic review of the research and evaluation evidence on diabetes prevention. CDC joined with federal researchers, state health officials, and healthcare industry representatives to review the evidence to identify the key features strongly associated with successful diabetes prevention—weight loss, greater physical activity, stress management, and supportive group interaction. This strong research base laid the basis for the program and was said to have been critical in obtaining support for the program.

All the evaluators noted that it usually takes a number of studies, rather than just one, to influence change in programs or policies. As one evaluator put it,

"the process by which evaluation influences change is iterative, messy, and complex. Policy changes do not occur as a direct result of an answer to an evaluation question; rather, a body of evaluation results, research, and other evidence influences policy and practice over time."

The evaluators explained that sharing what works with others is often the most direct action federal managers can take in decentralized programs where they do not have direct control of program activities conducted by others at the state or local level. In the public workforce system, states and localities set the amount of a voucher or Individual Training Account for individual jobseekers to obtain employment training, as well as how much guidance and direction counselors provide. ETA conducted a comparative effectiveness evaluation of how different service delivery models affected participation in counseling, training choices, expenditures, and impacts on participants' earnings. It found that providing more flexible, higher-value training awards was cost effective and had positive impacts on job seekers' long-term earnings. ETA then disseminated the results to state and local employment agencies to help inform their choice of programming.

HHS contracted for an evaluation review to identify programs effective in reducing teen pregnancy and sexually transmitted infections or sexual risk behaviors. The review rated the rigor of program impact studies and described the strength of evidence supporting different program models. Findings from the review were released along with grant announcements for the Office of Adolescent Health's Teen Pregnancy Prevention program, which supports the replication of evidence-based models and tests of additional models and innovative strategies. ACF evaluators disseminate their evaluation findings to researchers and practitioners through a listserv and events such as their annual Welfare Research and Evaluation Conference and Head Start's Biennial National Research Conference.[10] Since the 1990s these events have presented current research and evaluation for broad audiences of federal, state, and local government officials, practitioners, and researchers.

Since we have issued three reports outlining numerous areas of potential duplication and overlap in federal programs, it is encouraging to see that some agencies report making efforts to *streamline programs to reduce duplication.*[11] In these reviews, we identified the need for improved coordination and collaboration as well as better evaluation of performance

---

[10]See http://www.acf.hhs.gov/programs/opre.

[11]GAO, *2013 Annual Report: Actions Needed to Reduce Fragmentation, Overlap, and Duplication and Achieve Other Financial Benefits,* GAO-13-279SP (Washington, D.C.: Apr. 9, 2013); *2012 Annual Report: Opportunities to Reduce Duplication, Overlap, and Fragmentation, Achieve Savings, and Enhance Revenue,* GAO-12-342SP (Washington, D.C.: Feb. 28, 2012); and *Opportunities to Reduce Potential Duplication in Government Programs, Save Tax Dollars, and Enhance Revenue,* GAO-11-318SP (Washington, D.C.: Mar. 1, 2011).

and results to help inform decisions about how to streamline these programs. Evaluation studies, if carefully designed, can address specific questions about the comparative effectiveness of and extent of overlap among related programs. Common outcome measures are an important first step in comparing the effectiveness of alternative approaches. Collecting targeted data to compare the programs' actual coverage of specific localities or populations can clarify the extent of duplication and reveal opportunities for streamlining or better coordinating these programs.

For example, ETA used state data to "unbundle" the effects of Unemployment Insurance from other forms of assistance for low-income workers and families (such as SNAP and TANF) that were unavailable from analyses of national macroeconomic data. Officials noted that the evaluation, which looked at results during an earlier recession, helped the Congress understand the utility of the program and factored into their considerations on whether to extend benefits. The macroeconomic simulation models reaffirmed the value of these benefits as an automatic economic stabilizer during the latest recession.

Increasing Understanding of Program Performance

Managers reported that evaluations contributed to a *moderate or greater extent* to improving their understanding of program performance, such as in their

- assessing program effectiveness, value, or worth (80 percent);
- increasing understanding about the program or topic (76 percent); and
- supplementing or explaining performance results (75 percent).

The primary purpose of program and policy evaluations, of course, is to provide systematic evidence on how well a program is working, whether it is operating as intended or achieving its intended results. All the evaluators we interviewed indicated that each evaluation study added to a body of evidence and knowledge about the program that would influence policy over time. ACF evaluators noted that a 2012 report by the Advisory Committee on Head Start Research and Evaluation had drawn on a plethora of evidence about the program. The committee made use of a large body of knowledge on early childhood program interventions, including rigorous studies of Head Start and Early Head Start, to develop a number of recommendations for future research, policy, and practice. The Advisory Committee's recommendations were based on an intensive review and extensive deliberation on the implications of Head Start's history and unique features, as well as the current and evolving policy context for early childhood programs.

Evaluations reportedly also serve as a valuable supplement to routine performance monitoring. Managers reported that they contributed to a moderate or greater extent to developing or revising goals (72 percent) and supplementing or explaining performance results (75 percent). We have reported that evaluations can help explain the reasons for change (or lack of change) in program performance as well as measure more complex forms of performance than can feasibly be obtained on a routine basis.[12] ETA evaluators noted that performance measures are a good source of ideas for future research and evaluation, identifying areas that need attention. Moreover, they saw them as two prongs of evidence-based decision making; evaluation results are often integrated into program management through the use of performance measures. ACF evaluators indicated that the funds allocated for the evaluation of the Health Professions Opportunity Grant program led to the development of a management information system for the program. The National Implementation Evaluation is to assess implementation, system change, and outcomes in improving education and employment opportunities for TANF recipients and other low-income individuals. In setting up the program, the evaluators worked with the program staff and grantees to develop a reporting system to track grantee progress and inform the evaluation.

Allocating Program Resources

Fewer managers reported that evaluations contributed to a *moderate or greater extent* to *allocating resources within the program* (67 percent) than to improving program management or increasing understanding. Yet, in order to ensure that funds are directed toward activities most likely to significantly affect the HIV epidemic, CDC incorporated information from a national HIV-related resource allocation model to revise the way in which the agency funds health departments for HIV prevention. The new approach focused more on the highest-impact prevention strategies, informed in part by data on the costs and efficacy of key interventions for populations at various levels of risk for acquiring HIV.

---

[12]GAO, *Program Evaluation: Studies Helped Agencies Measure or Explain Program Performance,* GAO/GGD-00-204 (Washington, D.C.: Sept. 29, 2000).

GAO-13-570 Agency Use of Evaluation

Fewer managers also reported that evaluations contributed to a *moderate or greater extent* to *supporting program budget requests* (62 percent). This result is not surprising because, as we have pointed out, other factors and priorities influence the budget process.[13] OMB staff noted that evaluations do not typically address high-stakes issues, such as whether a program should be continued, but address lower-stakes issues, such as how program performance might be improved. However, several evaluators reported that their agencies included evaluation results in their budget justifications for OMB and the Congress.

Informing the Public

These federal managers' use of evaluations appears to be oriented more internally than externally. Few managers reported that evaluations contributed to informing the public about how programs were performing (36 percent rated it as small or no extent, and 26 percent reported that they had no basis to judge). This does not mean that they do not make their evaluation reports public; several agencies post them on their websites. It does imply that government transparency may still be a work in progress. For example, ETA posts evaluation evidence on best practices on a website targeted to the public workforce system for community colleges and state and local agencies to apply to their programs.[14] ETA has also made a public workforce dataset available to the public through Data.gov, the federal database repository, to encourage others to conduct research and evaluation on ETA programs.

Program Context Hinders an Evaluation's Use More Than Its Limitations or the Agency's Lack of Capacity

Our governmentwide survey asked federal managers who had had evaluations completed in the past 5 years to what extent 12 potential barriers had hindered their using evaluations in their agencies. We found that modest concerns related to program and policy context were reported to be greater barriers to an evaluation's use than problems with study quality or agency capacity or support for evaluation. Figure 2 summarizes their responses to all the barriers the survey posed.

---

[13]GAO, *Performance Budgeting; Observations on the Use of OMB's Program Assessment Rating Tool for the Fiscal Year 2004 Budget*, GAO-04-174 (Washington, D.C.: Jan. 30, 2004).

[14]See Labor's Workforce System Strategies, http://strategies.workforce3one.org/.

Figure 2: Managers Who Had Evaluations Report on the Extent to Which 12 Factors Hindered Their Use

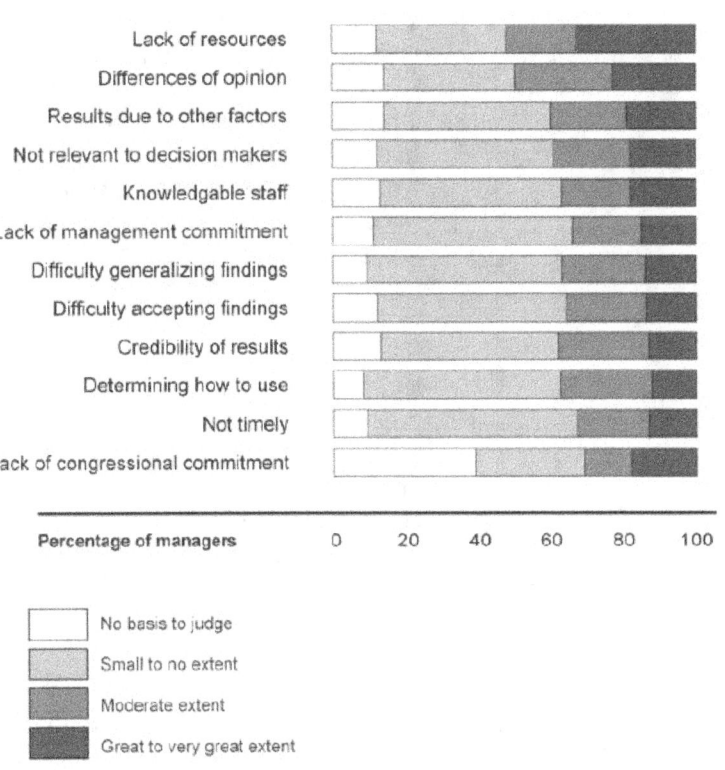

Lack of resources
Differences of opinion
Results due to other factors
Not relevant to decision makers
Knowledgable staff
Lack of management commitment
Difficulty generalizing findings
Difficulty accepting findings
Credibility of results
Determining how to use
Not timely
Lack of congressional commitment

Percentage of managers   0   20   40   60   80   100

☐ No basis to judge
▢ Small to no extent
▨ Moderate extent
▪ Great to very great extent

Source: GAO survey.

Note: These percentages are based on the response of managers who reported having program evaluations completed within the past 5 years.

Potential Barriers to Using Evaluation Related to Program and Policy Contexts

The only factor that more than one-fourth of the managers reported as having hindered the agency's use of evaluation to a *great or very great extent* was lack of resources to implement the evaluation findings (33 percent). The next most important barriers were also related to program context:

- difficulty resolving differences in opinion among internal or external program stakeholders (23 percent rated great or very great extent),
- difficulty distinguishing between the results produced by the program and the results caused by other factors (19 percent), and
- concern that the evaluation did not address issues that are important to decision-makers (18 percent).

Lack of Resources to Implement Findings

Among federal managers who had evaluations of their programs, policies, or projects, the barrier to their use most frequently identified was lack of resources (one-third rated a *great or very great extent*). This is not surprising given today's constrained federal budget resources; in a climate of budget reductions, agencies are hard pressed to argue for expanding or creating new programs. Some of the evaluators we interviewed noted that expensive or complicated programs, even if found to be effective, are unlikely to be adopted. Other evaluators thought it would be easier to defend a new investment if it were shown to be a cost-effective approach. Evaluators reported addressing this challenge by focusing on the cost-effectiveness of interventions and encouraging simpler program designs and effective program partnerships.

For example, CDC developed an optimal allocation tool to help state and local health departments determine how best to allocate their federal HIV prevention funds among interventions with the goal of preventing the greatest number of new cases of HIV. The evaluators reported that as program budgets remained constant or declined and as the number of persons living with HIV increased, health departments and local stakeholders became more accepting of transparent approaches to decision making, where the costs and benefits of decisions were made clear.

Some evaluators recommended a focus on identifying the key features that define an effective program in order to reduce the burden on grantees' attempting to implement a complex program and to improve their likelihood of success. The CDC Diabetes Prevention Program staff described four levers for scaling up a national program: quality standards with which to certify program sites, training to ensure that the program model would be implemented with fidelity, support and reimbursement for program sites, and participant engagement. The staff noted that having analyzed various options, they determined that it was important to develop a business model to operate—and obtain insurance reimbursement for—a new practical, scalable, and sustainable program outside the overburdened health care system.

Stakeholders' Differences of Opinion

Almost a quarter of federal managers perceived the effort to resolve differences of opinion among program stakeholders as a barrier to evaluation's use to a *great or very great extent*. The wide range of program stakeholders can include the Congress, executive branch officials, nonfederal program partners (state and local agencies and community-based organizations), program beneficiaries, and the policy research community. Their perspectives on evaluation results may differ

GAO-13-570 Agency Use of Evaluation

because of the complexity of study findings or differences in their policy opinions. One evaluator noted disagreements about what to do next when findings are not wholly positive or negative.

The CDC evaluators indicated that having a clear program outcome goal provided discipline and focus for basing a program's development on a review of research and evaluation, ensuring that they examined only approaches found effective in achieving the program goal. Evaluators also emphasized the importance of reaching out early to program staff to get buy-in on evaluation questions and establish ongoing communication throughout, building trusting relationships. In the end, however, evaluators said they recognized that sometimes political or ideological concerns override evaluation findings in decision making.

Other Factors' Effects on Results

Some federal managers we surveyed (19 percent) reported that difficulty distinguishing between results produced by the program and results caused by other factors was a *great or very great* barrier to evaluation use. Across the government, programs aim to achieve outcomes that they do not control, that are influenced by other programs or external social, economic, or environmental factors. Typically, this challenge is met by conducting a net impact evaluation that compares what occurred with an estimate of what would have occurred in the absence of the program.[15] However, these studies can be difficult to conduct and may not provide definitive results. Even when rigorous designs successfully exclude the influence of other factors, program officials may be reluctant to accept findings that do not match their expectations. Most of the evaluators we interviewed indicated that transparency regarding the evaluation's assumptions and how the data were obtained were important for gaining stakeholder buy-in to the credibility of the evaluation and its proposed use. In addition, they said that as program staff gained more understanding and familiarity with evaluation methods, they became more comfortable using their results.

However, in some circumstances, it may not be possible to construct evaluation designs that effectively isolate a program's impact. FNS evaluators explained, for example, that since many federal nutrition programs are entitlement programs that serve all eligible applicants, it is

---

[15]GAO, *Designing Evaluations: 2012 Revision*, GAO-12-208G (Washington, D.C.: January 2012).

difficult to find comparable nonparticipants with which to estimate the specific effects of receiving food assistance. In response to this challenge, evaluators said that they often evaluate, instead, the effects of modifications to entitlement programs. For example, FNS evaluators studied the effects of altering the way Summer Food Service Program benefits are delivered by using existing electronic benefits transfer technologies for SNAP and WIC (Special Supplemental Nutrition Program for Women, Infants, and Children) to provide $60 per month in food benefits to low-income children during the summer, when they do not receive school meals.

The Importance of Study Issues to Decision-makers

Some federal managers (18 percent) reported that the concern that an evaluation did not address issues that were important to decision-makers hindered its use to a *great or very great extent.* The evaluators we interviewed noted that evaluations were often not useful for budget justifications, for example, because they had been designed for a different, narrower purpose, such as assessing grantee performance or the effectiveness of a particular approach. As we pointed out in a previous report on how experienced agencies develop evaluation agendas, reaching out to key program and congressional stakeholders before developing proposals can help ensure that evaluations will be used effectively in management and legislative oversight.[16] Most of the evaluators indicated that their maintaining close communication with stakeholders helps them understand the issues that are important to program managers and policy makers and then design evaluations that will be useful to them.

For example, ETA evaluators described developing learning agendas with program staff: 5-year evaluation agendas that served as a strategic plan for conducting evaluations and revisiting them every 2 years to ensure that they continued to address the important issues. According to these evaluators, the process of setting these learning agendas has several benefits. Not only does joint planning create an opportunity for program staff to have ownership of and investment in the process; it also creates buy-in for the subsequent evaluations at executive and staff levels.

---

[16]GAO, *Program Evaluation: Experienced Agencies Follow a Similar Model for Prioritizing Research,* GAO-11-176 (Washington, D.C.: Jan. 14, 2011).

Potential Barriers Associated with Study Features or Agency Evaluation Capacity

Of seven potential barriers to use concerning the studies or an agency's capacity or support for using evaluations, none were generally considered significant by the 37 percent of federal managers who reported having evaluations:

- concern about the credibility (validity or reliability) of study results (49 percent rated *small or no extent*);
- difficulty generalizing the results to other persons or localities (53 percent);
- difficulty obtaining study results in time to be useful (58 percent);
- difficulty determining how to use evaluation findings to improve the program (54 percent);
- lack of staff knowledgeable about interpreting or analyzing program evaluation results (50 percent);
- difficulty accepting evaluation findings that do not conform to expectations (54 percent);
- lack of ongoing top executive commitment or support for using evaluation to make program or funding decisions (55 percent).

Study Characteristics

As we have reported before, an effective evaluation agenda aims to provide credible, timely answers to important policy and program questions.[17] Although many federal managers did not consider the credibility of study results (49 percent) or the ability to generalize the results to other persons or locations (53 percent) to be a significant barrier to use, the evaluators we interviewed generally emphasized the importance of having a body of strong evidence.

They said that they try to ensure *study credibility* by conducting rigorous, objective, independent research and that having several concurring studies helped build confidence in the findings and willingness to act on them. The evaluators said that research rigor was defined not by a particular choice of methods but by rigorous application of whatever method one chose: using "the right tool for the right situation." The evaluators did not raise the issue of the generalizability of results directly but did note the advantage of a body of evidence over a single study in showing that effects are consistent across different conditions and locations.

---

[17]GAO-11-176.

The majority of federal managers with evaluations (58 percent) reported that *not obtaining results in time to be useful* was a barrier to a small or no extent. The evaluators we interviewed indicated that evaluations might arrive too late to contribute to policy decisions for a variety of reasons. First, they noted that the pace of policy making is much quicker than the time it takes to conduct an evaluation and that they often faced a trade-off between obtaining robust results from careful study methods and providing timely answers to policy questions. They saw this as a particular disincentive for policy officials to conduct large evaluations. Evaluators described three different strategies for addressing this issue:

- providing managers with interim results or lessons learned about implementing program changes that they could use right away,
- assembling a body of evidence on a program or issue from which evaluators could respond to questions as they arise, and
- involving stakeholders in planning their evaluation agenda to ensure that they will have the information needed in the future.

Second, several evaluators singled out the reviews of data collection instruments required under the Paperwork Reduction Act of 1995 as adding at least a year to their evaluation planning, thus precluding the use of rigorous methods to produce quick policy responses.[18] Among other things, the act requires agencies to obtain public comment and secure OMB's approval before requiring members of the public to provide information. The purpose of these reviews includes improving the quality and practical utility of the information the federal government requests and reducing paperwork burden on the public. Prior to OMB's review, agencies are required, with some exceptions, to provide a 60-day public notice-and-comment period for each proposed information collection requirement not contained in a proposed rule. OMB's 60-day review process generally includes a second 30-day period of public comment. In addition, the public and OMB reviews are typically preceded by internal agency review, which also adds time to the evaluation planning process.

Others in the evaluation community have complained about the length of the review process, its application to quite small as well as large data collection efforts, and its discouraging effect on evaluation activity.[19] In

---

[18]44 U.S.C. §§ 3501–3520; 5 C.F.R. §§ 1320.1–1320.18.

[19]American Evaluation Association, *Comments on the Paperwork Reduction Act* (Fairhaven, Mass.: Dec. 16, 2009).

GAO-13-570 Agency Use of Evaluation

2010, OMB clarified the guidance for employing a streamlined "generic clearance" process intended for proposals to conduct multiple information collections using very similar methods.[20] In response to continued concerns, OMB staff recently met with federal evaluators to answer questions and discuss ways in which the review process might be streamlined.

The majority of federal managers (54 percent) reported that *determining how to use the findings to improve the program* was a barrier to a small or no extent. The evaluators we interviewed described circumstances in which study results might be tentative or open to interpretation, providing no clear recommendation for action. For example, a study might have a process component insufficient to help identify the reasons for poor performance. Broadly, all the evaluators we interviewed recommended developing a clear report message, distilling the findings into an easily digestible and usable form, and tailoring the message to the intended actor or audience. For example, CDC evaluators stated that to respond to frequent congressional and other stakeholder requests about the cost-effectiveness of their programs, they develop a one-page document that includes a succinct, clear message describing the value of their programs.

Agency Capacity and Support for Evaluation

We have previously reported on the importance of agency evaluation culture—sustaining a commitment to accountability and improving program performance—to supporting the regular conduct and use of evaluations.[21] As one might expect, most federal managers in offices that had access to evaluations reported that the presence of ongoing top executive commitment to using evaluations (55 percent rated small or no extent), staff knowledgeable about analyzing evaluation results (50 percent), and acceptance of findings that do not conform to expectations (54 percent) were not significant barriers to evaluation use.

Indeed, all the evaluators we interviewed pointed to the research and policy expertise of their evaluation staff and their agency leadership's

---

[20]OMB, *Paperwork Reduction Act—Generic Clearances,* Memorandum for the Heads of Executive Departments and Agencies and Independent Regulatory Agencies (Washington, D.C.: May 28, 2010).

[21]GAO, *Program Evaluation: An Evaluation Culture and Collaborative Partnerships Help Build Agency Capacity,* GAO-03-454 (Washington, D.C.: May 2, 2003).

commitment to evaluation as key to facilitating the use of their evaluation results. The ACF, ETA, and FNS evaluation offices, and many of their staff, have been producing evaluations for decades. The leadership of these agencies also demonstrates support for evaluation through allocating funding for evaluation and the operations of these offices and forming close working relationships with their evaluators. At the department level, Labor's Deputy Secretary asked each component agency to substantiate its congressional budget justifications and operating plans with performance data and evaluation information. CDC's Office of the Associate Director for Program described working with the program offices to integrate evaluation findings into their budget justifications for OMB and congressional appropriators. An evaluator we interviewed noted, however, that political staff turnover can inhibit developing leadership support for evaluation because it is hard to gain support for a study whose results may arrive after staff have left the agency.

Some of the evaluators we interviewed noted that differences between evaluators and program staff in mission, world view, and pace sometimes made it difficult to gain program staff support for or interest in longer-term studies or for the notion of continuous program improvement. They pointed out that while evaluation staff are interested in assessing long-term program impacts, program staff are more interested in shorter-term projects. Evaluations can be a burden for program offices, given their workload, and program staff may discount negative findings unless they understand how they were derived.

The evaluators generally said that diligent outreach, effective relationships and trust, evaluation training, and developing audience-friendly formats for presenting results help mitigate these challenges. Evaluators described a variety of efforts—formal and informal—to engage regularly with program staff: providing technical assistance and tools for performance monitoring and evaluation, building staff understanding of the logic of evaluation, and improving evaluators' understanding of program and policy issues and information needs. ETA evaluators brief program staff on completed evaluations' evidence and findings. Evaluation offices throughout Labor host two to three seminars a month to discuss both substantive and methodological issues to improve staff's awareness and knowledge of evaluation.

For example, the CDC Office of the Associate Director for Program developed a template for all nonresearch domestic Funding Opportunity Announcements to, among other things, ensure clarity for applicants on the program's purpose and scope and provide a strong evaluation approach that aligns with the program's purpose, activities, and outcomes. The template also requires applicants and CDC programs to indicate how findings will be made available and used, helping to ensure that evaluations align with the CDC program's work plan and produce findings that will be used in planning and other decision making.

Decentralized programs, whose control over program activities is state and local, can restrict the ability of federal program officials to act on evaluation results. Officials must convince state or local program officials, grantees, or others in industry to adopt program evaluation findings and recommendations. Evaluators explained that program partners and grantees who deliver program services but are not directly managed by federal staff may lack evaluation capacity and may be reluctant to use evaluation findings to change their activities without a clear mandate to do so. Some evaluators described using carrots and sticks to obtain program staff and partners' interest and involvement in their evaluations. The allocation of funds for evaluation and requirements in grants to conduct evaluation helped gain program partners' interest and involvement in the evaluations and their results. Evaluators reported disseminating evaluation results and program guidance to local service providers, engaging with intermediary organizations such as professional associations to disseminate their evaluation results, and working directly with program staff to help grantees implement effective program approaches.

Managers' Limited Knowledge of Congressional Support for Evaluation

Only 18 percent of managers reported that lack of ongoing congressional commitment to use evaluation to make program or funding decisions was a barrier to use to a great or very great extent; however, more (39 percent) reported not being able to judge whether this was a barrier. Of course, agency staff on their own can implement some evaluation recommendations, whereas others may require legislative changes. In addition, agency managers, especially those not in the SES, may have quite limited contact with congressional staff and members; our interviews with evaluators indicated few such contacts. One evaluator stated that, for the most part, agency officials conduct formal briefings for the Congress in a tense, high-stakes environment; they lack the opportunity for informal discussion. To help improve the usefulness of agency performance information to Congress, GPRAMA significantly enhances requirements for agencies to consult with Congress when establishing or adjusting their strategic plans and agency priority goals. We recently issued a guide to assist Congress in ensuring the usefulness of these consultations and in using performance information in various legislative and oversight activities.[22]

Agencies may strategically plan work to gain congressional attention. ETA planned a survey to coincide with the anniversary of the Family Medical Leave Act of 1993 so that policy makers could use results in reexamining the program. CDC assembled a body of research and evaluation evidence supporting diabetes prevention that resulted in congressional support and authorizing legislation for the National Diabetes Prevention Program. However, as discussed previously, several responses to our survey suggest that many federal managers are focused relatively internally on their programs rather than on the broader policy environment and may be unfamiliar with congressional concerns.

Lessons for Facilitating Agencies' Use of Evaluation Results

The evaluators we interviewed emphasized three basic strategies to facilitate evaluation's influencing program management and policy:

- demonstrate leadership support of evaluation for accountability and program improvement,
- build a strong body of evidence, and
- engage stakeholders throughout the evaluation process.

Demonstrate Leadership Support for Evaluation for Program Accountability and Improvement

Agency leadership can both provide support for conducting evaluations and encourage a culture of experimentation and continuous improvement. During the administrations of Presidents George W. Bush and Barack Obama, OMB has encouraged agencies formally and informally to expand their evaluation efforts and to use evidence and rigorous evaluation in budget, management, and policy decisions to improve government effectiveness. In 2002–07, OMB used the Program Assessment Rating Tool (PART) to bring assessments of program results explicitly into the budget formulation process. By asking whether a program had undergone regular independent program evaluations, PART

---

[22]GAO, *Managing for Results: A Guide for Using the GPRA Modernization Act to Help Inform Congressional Decision Making*, GAO-12-621SP (Washington, D.C.: June 15, 2012).

sent the message that program assessment and evaluation was an important management tool.[23]

In October 2009, OMB announced an initiative to strengthen federal program evaluation by posting information online on all agencies' planned and ongoing impact evaluations, establishing an interagency group to promote the sharing of evaluation expertise, and funding some rigorous new agency impact evaluations and capacity strengthening efforts.[24] In May 2012, OMB asked agencies to demonstrate the use of evidence and evaluation throughout their budget submissions, encouraged the designation of a high-level official responsible for program evaluation, and announced a number of forums for information development and sharing to improve agency use of evidence.[25] In interviews, OMB staff noted that agencies vary so much that they cannot deliver a top-down evaluation mandate on what to do; instead, they work with OMB Resource Management Officers and agency staff on how to use evaluations and institutionalize evaluations "as part of agencies' DNA."

Nevertheless, as OMB staff observed, the federal government's capacity and support for evaluation vary widely. The agencies where we conducted interviews were selected for their evaluation capacity and, naturally, demonstrated leadership support for conducting and using evaluations. Several evaluators reported that their deputy secretary and other senior officials strongly emphasized the use of evidence for decision making and asked for performance and evaluation data in budget justifications and operating plans. In addition, these five agencies gave the evaluation offices responsibility for promoting evaluation capacity and providing an organizational framework for planning and conducting

---

[23]GAO, *Performance Budgeting: PART Focuses Attention on Program Performance, but More Can Be Done to Engage Congress,* GAO-06-28 (Washington, D.C.: Oct. 28, 2005).

[24]OMB, *Increased Emphasis on Program Evaluations,* M-10-01, Memorandum for the Heads of Executive Departments and Agencies (Washington, D.C.: The White House, Oct. 7, 2009).

[25]OMB, *Use of Evidence and Evaluation in the 2014 Budget,* M-12-14, Memorandum to the Heads of Executive Departments and Agencies (Washington, D.C.: The White House, May 18, 2012).

evaluation, similar to that recommended by the American Evaluation Association.[26]

Labor created the Office of the Chief Evaluation Officer in 2010 to coordinate and provide guidance to evaluations conducted throughout the department. Also in 2010, CDC created the Office of the Associate Director for Program to promote continuous program improvement and provide direction and consultation to program planning, performance measurement, and evaluation conducted by individual CDC centers. In November 2012, ACF established a formal evaluation policy that reaffirms its commitment to conducting evaluation and using evidence from evaluations to inform policy and practice. The policy describes the procedures and policies by which ACF seeks to promote the principles of rigor, relevance, transparency, independence, and ethics in conducting evaluation.[27]

The ACF and FNS evaluation offices have a long history of supporting their agencies' policy making process and described having close communication with and support from their agency leadership. For example, the Associate Administrator heading FNS's evaluation office reported participating regularly in discussions of program and policy changes with the Administrator. ACF OPRE has also partnered with HHS's Office of the Assistant Secretary for Planning and Evaluation to research the best techniques for disseminating evaluation results.

Build a Strong Body of Evidence

Strong evidence may include descriptive research, clinical trials, evaluations of innovative practices, survey statistics, performance data, case studies, and program administrative data. All the evaluators indicated that attention to evaluation rigor and quality was critical, no matter the methods used. They noted that randomized experiments, although extremely powerful for assessing program net impact, were not always necessary or feasible and that it was important to use the right tool for the right situation.

---

[26]American Evaluation Association, *An Evaluation Roadmap for a More Effective Government* (Fairhaven, Mass.: 2010), http://www.eval.org.

[27]ACF, *Evaluation Policy* (Washington, D.C.: November 2012), http://www.acf.hhs.gov/programs/opre/resource/acf-evaluation-policy.

These evaluators drew on systematic literature reviews, a portfolio of studies and program data, and an agency's many years of experience with scaling up national programs to develop a knowledge base over time. A body of evidence was considered more valuable than a single study because multiple studies with similar results strengthens confidence in their conclusions, and a body of information can yield answers to a variety of different questions, whenever stakeholders pose them.

These evaluators pointed out that they rarely based decisions on a single study. Individual evaluation studies typically do not simply identify whether a program works but, rather, assess the effects of an individual program or intervention on specific domains (such as employment or educational attainment) for the specific populations and conditions studied. Programs found effective in their initial development stage need to be reevaluated when implemented by someone other than the program developer under less auspicious conditions. Accumulating a body of evidence on an issue was also considered important because no one study or form of data can answer all questions. It is also a strategy for ensuring that information is available for input to fast-breaking policy discussions.

Engage Program Stakeholders throughout an Evaluation

All the evaluation officials we interviewed stressed the importance of developing good relationships with program stakeholders and involving them in evaluations to promote their use. They involved stakeholders throughout the evaluation planning, execution, and reporting stages to gain their buy-in on the relevance and credibility of evaluation findings.

Developing Relationships and Trust

Evaluators recommended conducting outreach to and maintaining close communication with program managers and policymakers in order to understand the issues they face and design evaluations that will be helpful to them. Evaluators at ACF, ETA, and FNS consulted with their program offices and other stakeholders to ensure that their evaluation agendas addressed policy and management information needs. Consulting with program staff throughout an evaluation was said to help ensure a more trusting relationship and a greater willingness to hear not-so-good news when the evaluation results came in. Program staff may be unwilling to accept negative findings because they have a vested interest in trying to make the program work. But this can be countered if staff understand the logic of the evaluation or if the study provides information on barriers that might be overcome.

Some evaluators noted that it was important to find the right balance of proximity and independence between program and evaluation staff. Evaluations have to be objective and independent enough that readers have faith in their findings and conclusions, but stretching independence too far risks the irrelevance of results to the policy and program staff. Others warned that if evaluators are located within program offices, then their studies may get buried and important findings may not reach the leadership. ACF's evaluation policy highlights the importance of obtaining stakeholder input to evaluation priorities and planning while protecting independence in evaluation design, conduct, and analysis.

Building Evaluation Capacity

The evaluators described providing assistance, training, and incentives to program staff and service providers to conduct and use evaluations. Evaluation offices provided technical assistance themselves or through contractors for evaluations conducted by program offices or grantees and for performance measurement systems. Both Labor's CEO and the CDC OADPG developed tools and guidance for evaluation planning and use. The CEO described developing checklists for implementation and effectiveness evaluations, method guidelines, and templates for preparing data collection packages for OMB's review. They also reported holding two or three seminars a month on evaluation methods or individual studies for both evaluation and program staff. OADPG provided evaluation guidelines and recommendations, and a grant announcement template for focusing an evaluation's purpose and intended use. OADPG also funds an evaluation fellows program to increase evaluation capacity in the centers. ACF sponsors an annual Welfare Research and Evaluation Conference of researchers, state and local program administrators, practitioners, and federal officials and policymakers who meet and learn about research on and experience with family self-sufficiency and social welfare programs and policies. ACF and ETA evaluators noted that embedding evaluation in grant programs serves as a significant incentive for state and local agency staff to get involved in and use evaluations.

Disseminating Results

A key strategy recommended for promoting the use of evaluation findings was to distill them to make them digestible and usable and to proactively disseminate them. In addition to posting findings on agency websites, evaluators may tailor a message to fit various audiences such as federal agency program offices and policy makers, state and local agencies, and local program affiliates. It can be very important to provide program staff with interim results or lessons from early implementation to ensure timely data for program decisions, as well as help them integrate findings into their program budget justifications.

ETA conducts briefings for agency staff on each evaluation as it is completed and packages lessons learned from evaluations as "promising practices" and guidance to local program affiliates in private industry through the Workforce Systems Strategies website.[28] ACF uses regular research conferences and a listserv to disseminate evaluation findings to intermediary professional organizations that can be especially influential for program practitioners' adoption of those findings. In the diabetes prevention program, CDC provided an unusual example of leveraging and coordinating the resources of several nongovernmental program partners to implement a national program based on evaluation findings.

Concluding Observations

Agencies' lack of evaluations may be the greatest barrier to their ability to inform program management and policy making. Four-fifths of federal managers who had evaluations reported that they contributed to implementing changes to improve program management or performance. Moreover, the greatest barrier to evaluation use was having insufficient resources to implement their findings rather than having difficulty accepting them or determining how to use them. Yet, just over a third of federal managers reported that an evaluation had been completed in the past 5 years on any of the programs, operations, or projects that they were involved in. We believe this gap represents lost opportunities for agencies to identify ways to improve federal government efficiency and effectiveness.

Seeking out in advance the interests and concerns of key program stakeholders, including the Congress, can help ensure that agency evaluations provide the information necessary for effective management and congressional oversight. Two of the barriers to evaluation use managers most frequently cited in our survey concerned addressing issues important to decision makers and resolving differences of opinion among stakeholders. Yet, nearly 40 percent of managers who had evaluations reported that they did not know whether lack of ongoing congressional commitment to using evaluations was a barrier, and some of the evaluators we interviewed reported few congressional consultations in planning evaluations. Consultation with congressional stakeholders in developing evaluation agendas is important to help ensure that agency evaluations meet their information needs and inform decisions.

---

[28]See http://strategies.workforce3one.org.

Comprehensive program evaluations that examine the coverage and effectiveness of a cluster of federal programs and policies aimed at achieving similar outcomes could be key in coordinating and streamlining programs so as to reduce duplication and overlap. Over the past 3 years, we have identified numerous areas of fragmentation, overlap, or duplication in federal programs and activities. Carefully designed evaluation of performance and results for clusters of related programs—adoption of common measures and direct assessment of their overlap—could reveal ways to streamline, consolidate, or better coordinate those programs.

Agency Comments

We requested comments on a draft of this report from the Secretaries of Agriculture, Health and Human Services, and Labor and the Director of the Office of Management and Budget. The agencies and OMB staff provided technical comments that we incorporated as appropriate.

We are sending copies of this report to the Secretaries of Agriculture, Health and Human Services, and Labor; to the Director of the Office of Management and Budget; and to appropriate congressional committees. The report is also available at no charge on the GAO website at http://www.gao.gov.

If you or your staff have any questions about this report, please contact me at (202) 512-2700 or kingsburyn@gao.gov. Contact points for our Office of Congressional Relations and Office of Public Affairs may be found on the last page of this report. Staff who made key contributions to this report are listed in appendix II.

Nancy R. Kingsbury

Nancy Kingsbury, Ph.D.
Managing Director
Applied Research and Methods

Appendix I: Methodology for Federal Managers Survey

We administered a web-based questionnaire on organizational performance and management issues to a stratified random sample of 4,391 persons from a population of approximately 148,300 mid-level and upper-level civilian managers and supervisors working in the 24 executive branch agencies covered by the Chief Financial Officers Act of 1990 (CFO Act), as amended. The sample was drawn from the Office of Personnel Management's (OPM) Central Personnel Data File (CPDF) as of March 2012, using file designators indicating performance of managerial and supervisory functions. The sample was stratified by agency and by whether the manager or supervisor was a member of the Senior Executive Service (SES) or not. The management levels covered general schedule (GS) or equivalent schedules in other pay plans at levels comparable to GS-13 through GS-15 and career SES, or equivalent. In reporting the questionnaire data, when we use the term "governmentwide" or the phrase "across the federal government" we are referring to these 24 CFO Act executive branch agencies, and when we use the terms "federal managers" and "managers" we are referring to both managers and supervisors.

The questionnaire was designed to obtain the observations and perceptions of respondents on various aspects of such results-oriented management topics as the presence and use of performance measures, hindrances to measuring performance and using performance information, agency climate, and program evaluation use. In addition, to address implementation of GPRAMA, the questionnaire included a section requesting respondents' views on various provisions of GPRAMA, such as cross-agency priority goals, agency priority goals, and quarterly performance reviews.

This survey is similar to surveys we have conducted four times previously at the 24 CFO Act agencies—1997, 2000, 2003, and 2007—except that the questions on GPRAMA provisions and program evaluation use were new in 2013. The 1997 survey was conducted as part of the work we did in response to a GPRA requirement that we report on implementation of the act. The 2000, 2003, and 2007 surveys were designed to update the results from each of the previous surveys.[1] We conducted pretests of the new questions with federal managers in several of the 24 CFO Act agencies.

Most of the items on the questionnaire were closed-ended, meaning that depending on the particular item, respondents could choose one or more response categories or rate the strength of their perception on a 5-point "extent" scale ranging from "to no extent" at the low end of the scale to "to a very great extent" at the high end. On most items, respondents also had an option of choosing the response category "no basis to judge/not applicable." A few items had yes, no, or do not know options for respondents.

To administer the survey, an e-mail was sent to managers in the sample that notified them of the survey's availability on the GAO website and included instructions on how to access and complete the survey. Managers in the sample who did not respond to the initial notice were sent up to four subsequent e-mail reminders and follow-up phone calls asking them to participate in the survey. From the 4,391 managers selected for this survey, we found that 266 of the sampled managers had retired, separated, died, or otherwise left the agency or had some other reason that excluded them from the population of interest. We received usable questionnaires from 2,762 sample respondents, or about 69 percent of the remaining eligible sample. The response rate across the 24 agencies ranged from 57 percent to 88 percent.

The overall survey results can be generalized to the population of managers as described above at each of the 24 agencies and governmentwide. The responses of each eligible sample member who provided a usable questionnaire were weighted in the analyses to account statistically for all members of the population. All results are subject to some uncertainty or sampling error as well as nonsampling

---

[1]For information on the design and administration of the four earlier surveys, see GAO, *The Government Performance and Results Act: 1997 Governmentwide Implementation Will Be Uneven*, GAO/GGD-97-109 (Washington, D.C.: June 2, 1997); *Managing for Results: Federal Managers' Views on Key Management Issues Vary Widely across Agencies*, GAO-01-592 (Washington, D.C.: May 25, 2001); *Results-Oriented Government: GPRA Has Established a Solid Foundation for Achieving Greater Results*, GAO-04-38 (Washington, D.C.: Mar. 10, 2004); and *Government Performance: Lessons Learned for the Next Administration on Using Performance Information to Improve Results*, GAO-08-1026T (Washington, D.C.: July 24, 2008).

error. The governmentwide percentage estimates based on our sample from 2012 presented in this report have 95 percent confidence intervals within plus or minus 4 percentage points of the estimate itself for the initial question about whether an evaluation had been completed and within 5 to 6 percentage points for subsequent questions about use of those evaluations. An online e-supplement shows the questions asked on the survey along with the percentage estimates and associated 95 percent confidence intervals for each item for each agency and governmentwide.[2] For additional details on the survey methodology, see our report summarizing our body of work on the implementation of GPRAMA.[3]

---

[2]GAO, *Managing for Results: 2013 Federal Managers Survey on Organizational Performance and Management Issues,* GAO-13-519SP (Washington, D.C.: June 2013).

[3]GAO, *Managing for Results: Executive Branch Should More Fully Implement the GPRA Modernization Act to Address Pressing Governance Challenges,* GAO-13-518 (Washington, D.C.: June 26, 2013).

Appendix II: GAO Contact and Staff Acknowledgments

GAO Contact	Nancy Kingsbury, (202) 512-2700 or kingsburyn@gao.gov
Staff Acknowledgments	In addition to the contact named above, Stephanie Shipman (Assistant Director), Thomas Beall, Valerie Caracelli, Thomas Clarke, Stuart Kaufman, Jamila Kennedy, Penny Pickett, Mark Ramage, and Paul Teicher made key contributions to this report.

References

Administration for Children and Families. *Evaluation Policy*. Washington, D.C.: Department of Health and Human Services, November 2012.

American Evaluation Association. *Comments on the Paperwork Reduction Act*. Fairhaven, Mass.: December 16, 2009.

American Evaluation Association. *An Evaluation Roadmap for a More Effective Government*. Fairhaven, Mass.: September 2010. www.eval.org/EPTF.asp.

Cousins, J. Bradley and Kenneth A. Leithwood. "Current Empirical Research on Evaluation Utilization," *Review of Educational Research*, 56:3 (1986): 331–64.

Hatry, Harry P., and others. *How Federal Programs Use Outcome Information: Opportunities for Federal Managers*. Washington, D.C.: IBM Endowment for the Business of Government, 2003.

The Lewin Group. *Getting the Most out of Evaluations: A Guide to Successful Evaluation Utilization*. Washington, D.C.: U.S. Department of Health and Human Services, June 30, 2009.

Macoubrie, J., and C. Harrison. *Human Services Research Dissemination: What Works?* OPRE Report 2013-09. Washington, D.C.: Office of Planning, Research, and Evaluation, Administration for Children and Families, U.S. Department of Health and Human Services, 2013.

Macoubrie, J., and C. Harrison. *The Value-Added Research Dissemination Framework*. OPRE Report 2013-10. Washington, D.C.: Office of Planning, Research, and Evaluation, Administration for Children and Families, U.S. Department of Health and Human Services, 2013.

Mark, Melvin M., Gary T. Henry, and George Julnes. *Evaluation: An Integrated Framework for Understanding, Guiding, and Improving Public and Nonprofit Policies and Programs*. San Francisco, Calif.: Jossey-Bass, 2000.

Mathison, Sandra, ed. *Encyclopedia of Evaluation*. Thousand Oaks, Calif.: Sage Publications, 2005.

Nutley, Sandra M., Isabel Walter, and Huw T. O. Davies. *Using Evidence: How Research Can Inform Public Services*. Bristol, U.K.: The Policy Press, 2007.

Office of Management and Budget. *Increased Emphasis on Program Evaluations*. Memorandum for the Heads of Executive Departments and Agencies, M-10-01. Washington, D.C.: The White House, Oct. 7, 2009.

Office of Management and Budget. *Paperwork Reduction Act—Generic Clearances*, Memorandum for the Heads of Executive Departments and Agencies and Independent Regulatory Agencies. Washington, D.C.: The White House, May 28, 2010.

Office of Management and Budget. *Use of Evidence and Evaluation in the 2014 Budget*, Memorandum to the Heads of Executive Departments and Agencies, M-12-14. Washington, D.C.: The White House, May 18, 2012.

Ottoson, J. M. "Knowledge-for-Action Theories in Evaluation: Knowledge Utilization, Diffusion, Implementation, Transfer, and Translation." In J. M. Ottoson and P. Hawe, eds. *Knowledge Utilization, Diffusion, Implementation, Transfer, and Translation: Implications for Evaluation. New Directions for Evaluation*, 124 (2009): 7–20.

Patton, Michael Quinn. *Utilization-Focused Evaluation*, 4th ed. Los Angeles, Calif.: Sage, 2008.

Prewitt, Kenneth, Thomas A. Schwandt, and Miron L. Straf, eds. *Using Science as Evidence in Public Policy*. National Research Council, Division of Behavioral and Social Sciences and Education. Washington, D.C.: National Academies Press, 2012.

Weiss, Carol H., and others. "The Fairy Godmother and Her Warts: Making the Dream of Evidence-Based Policy Come True." *American Journal of Evaluation*, 29:1 (March 2008): 29–47.

Related GAO Products

Managing for Results: 2013 Federal Managers Survey on Organizational Performance and Management Issues. GAO-13-519SP. Washington, D.C.: June 2013.

Managing for Results: Executive Branch Should More Fully Implement the GPRA Modernization Act to Address Pressing Governance Challenges. GAO-13-518. Washington, D.C.: June 26, 2013.

Managing for Results: Leading Practices Should Guide the Continued Development of Performance.gov. GAO-13-517. Washington, D.C.: June 6, 2013.

Managing for Results: Agencies Should More Fully Develop Priority Goals under the GPRA Modernization Act. GAO-13-174. Washington, D.C.: April 19, 2013.

Managing for Results: Agencies Have Elevated Performance Management Leadership Roles, but Additional Training Is Needed. GAO-13-356. Washington, D.C.: April 16, 2013.

2013 Annual Report: Actions Needed to Reduce Fragmentation, Overlap, and Duplication and Achieve Other Financial Benefits. GAO-13-279SP. Washington, D.C.: April 9, 2013.

Managing for Results: Data-Driven Performance Reviews Show Promise but Agencies Should Explore How to Involve Other Relevant Agencies. GAO-13-228. Washington, D.C.: February 27, 2013.

Managing for Results: A Guide for Using the GPRA Modernization Act to Help Inform Congressional Decision Making. GAO-12-621SP. Washington, D.C.: June 15, 2012.

Managing for Results: GAO's Work Related to the Interim Crosscutting Priority Goals under the GPRA Modernization Act. GAO-12-620R. Washington, D.C.: May 31, 2012.

2012 Annual Report: Opportunities to Reduce Duplication, Overlap, and Fragmentation, Achieve Savings, and Enhance Revenue. GAO-12-342SP. Washington, D.C.: February 28, 2012.

Designing Evaluations: 2012 Revision. GAO-12-208G. Washington, D.C.: January 2012.

Performance Measurement and Evaluation: Definitions and Relationships. GAO-11-646SP. Washington, D.C.: May 2011.

Employment and Training Administration: More Actions Needed to Improve Transparency and Accountability of Its Research Program. GAO-11-285. Washington, D.C.: March 15, 2011.

Opportunities to Reduce Potential Duplication in Government Programs, Save Tax Dollars, and Enhance Revenue. GAO-11-318SP. Washington, D.C.: March 1, 2011.

Program Evaluation: Experienced Agencies Follow a Similar Model for Prioritizing Research. GAO-11-176. Washington, D.C.: January 14, 2011.

Employment and Training Administration: Increased Authority and Accountability Could Improve Research Program. GAO-10-243. Washington, D.C.: January 29, 2010.

Government Performance: Lessons Learned for the Next Administration on Using Performance Information to Improve Results. GAO-08-1026T. Washington, D.C.: July 24, 2008.

Performance Budgeting: PART Focuses Attention on Program Performance, but More Can Be Done to Engage Congress. GAO-06-28. Washington, D.C.: October 28, 2005.

Managing for Results: Enhancing Agency Use of Performance Information for Management Decision Making. GAO-05-927. Washington, D.C.: September 9, 2005.

Performance Budgeting: Observations on the Use of OMB's Program Assessment Rating Tool for the Fiscal Year 2004 Budget. GAO-04-174. Washington, D.C.: January 30, 2004.

Program Evaluation: An Evaluation Culture and Collaborative Partnerships Help Build Agency Capacity. GAO-03-454. Washington, D.C.: May 2, 2003.

Program Evaluation: Studies Helped Agencies Measure or Explain Program Performance. GAO/GGD-00-204. Washington, D.C.: September 29, 2000.

www.ingramcontent.com/pod-product-compliance
Lightning Source LLC
Chambersburg PA
CBHW080630290526

45790CB00007B/3003